Wild Weather

REVISED AND UPDATED

Catherine Chambers

Heinemann Library
Chicago, Illinois

© 2002, 2007 Heinemann Library
a division of Reed Elsevier Inc.
Chicago, Illinois

Customer Service 888-454-2279

Visit our website at www.heinemannraintree.com

Designed by Steve Mead and Q2A Creative
Maps by Paul Bale
Printed in China by South China Printing Company

11 10
10 9 8 7 6 5 4 3

New edition ISBN: 978-1-403-49579-2 (hardcover)
                    978-1-403-49588-4 (paperback)

The Library of Congress has cataloged the first edition as follows:
Chambers, Catherine, 1954-
 Hurricane / Catherine Chambers.
       p. cm. -- (Wild weather)
Summary: Describes how hurricanes are formed, how they are measured, the harmful and beneficial impact of these storms, and the impact on humans, animals, and plants.
Includes bibliographical references and index.
 ISBN 1-58810-651-9 (HC), 1-4034-0114-4 (Pbk)
 1. Hurricanes--Juvenile literature. 2. Hurricanes – Physiological effect--
Juvenile literature. [1. Hurricanes] I. Title. II. Series.
 QC944.2 .C478 2002
 551.55'2--dc21
                          2002000821

Acknowledgments

The author and publishers are grateful to the following for permission to reproduce copyright material: AP Photo/Mark Saltz/STR p22,Associated Press pp4, 9, 13, Corbis pp5, 11, 20, 24, 27, 29, James Nielsen/AFP/Getty Images p23, PA Photos p21, Panos p28, Photodisc p25, Joe Raedle/Getty Images p18, Reuters/Corbis p14, Rex Features pp15, 19, 26, Robert Harding Picture Library p12, Royalty Free/Corbis pp7, 16, Science Photo Library p10, Mar Torres/AFP/Getty Images p17.

Cover photograph of palm trees during Hurricane Wilma in 2005 reproduced with permission of Daniel Aguilar/Reuters/Corbis.

The publishers would like to thank Mark Rogers and the Met Office for their assistance with the preparation of this book.

Every effort has been made to contact copyright holders of any material reproduced in this book. Any omissions will be rectified in subsequent printings if notice is given to the publisher.

The paper used to print this book comes from sustainable sources.

Some words are shown in bold, **like this**. You can find out what they mean by looking in the glossary.

Contents

What Is a Hurricane?

A hurricane is a huge storm that builds up over an **ocean**. Strong winds hit the land. Swirling clouds bring heavy rain.

■ *The wind is very powerful in a hurricane.*

■ *Hurricanes can cause a lot of damage.*

Hurricane winds can blow roofs off and smash windows. They snap trees and flatten **crops**. Streets and homes can be flooded by heavy rain or huge sea waves.

Where Do Hurricanes Happen?

Hurricanes happen in regions called the **Tropics**. The Tropics are hot because the heat of the Sun is stronger. Hurricanes are called "typhoons" in some places.

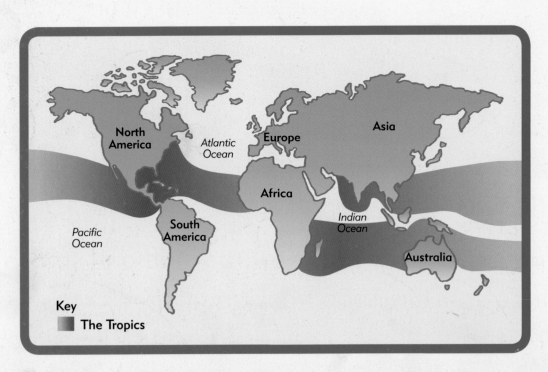

Key

  The Tropics

■ *The areas in blue on this map show where hurricanes happen.*

■ *This country lies in a **hurricane zone**.*

This place lies in the Tropics. Very strong hurricanes happen here because it is close to warm **oceans**. Warm oceans help hurricanes to form.

How Do Hurricanes Form?

Masses of air are always moving. A warm mass of air usually rises. This makes a low **pressure** area. A cold mass sinks. This makes high pressure. Winds blow from high pressure to low pressure.

■ *This diagram shows how masses of air are moved by the wind.*

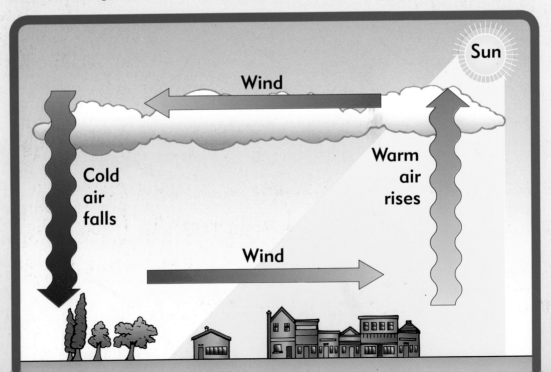

Sun

Wind

Cold air falls

Warm air rises

Wind

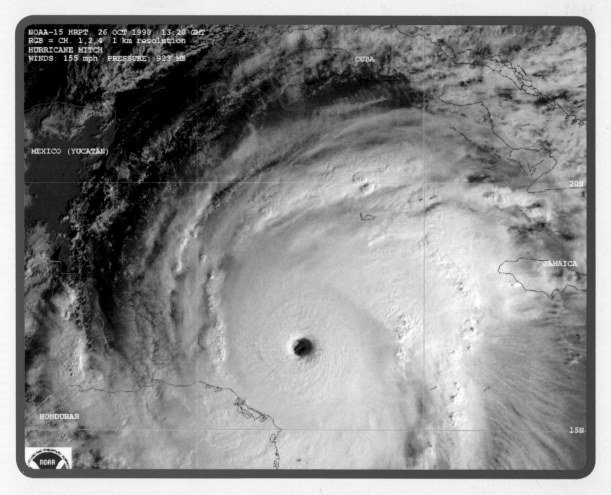

NOAA-15 HRPT 26 OCT 1998 13:20 GMT
RGB = CH. 1,2,4 1 km resolution
HURRICANE MITCH
WINDS: 155 mph PRESSURE: 923 MB

CUBA

MEXICO (YUCATAN)

20N

JAMAICA

HONDURAS

15N

NOAA

■ *This photograph shows a hurricane from space.*

Hurricanes happen when air rises quickly over warm **oceans** in the **Tropics**. This makes a low pressure area. Strong winds rush in from high pressure areas. They form a **spiral** of wind and clouds around an area of calm air.

What Do Hurricanes Do?

Hurricanes form over the **ocean**. Hurricane winds are very powerful. The winds blow the ocean waters into huge waves. Heavy rain falls from huge, dark clouds.

■ *Hurricanes can damage and sink boats.*

■ *Houses on the coast can be in danger.*

Most hurricanes blow on to tropical **coasts**. As a hurricane blows over the land, it gets less powerful. The hurricane can still do a lot of damage.

What Are Hurricanes Like?

Sometimes hurricane winds blow through towns and cities. They uproot trees and blow the roofs off buildings. It is too windy for people to go outside.

■ *It is dangerous to go outside in a hurricane.*

■ *The heavy rain can flood roads.*

Hurricanes also bring heavy rain. They drop the water they have picked up from the **ocean** onto the land. This often causes **floods**.

Harmful Hurricanes

A hurricane **storm surge** has hit this **shore**.
A storm surge is a huge wave pushed by the strong winds. The wave **floods** the shore.
These boats have been carried on to the land.

■ *These boats have been damaged by a hurricane.*

■ *This airport has been destroyed.*

Hurricanes damage roads, railroads, bridges, and airports. This makes it difficult for rescuers to reach people after a hurricane.

Hurricane in Mexico

This is Cancun in Mexico. Eastern Mexico faces the warm Caribbean Sea. People go there on vacation. Mexico gets a lot of hurricanes.

■ *People love to go to the beach in Cancun when the weather is good.*

■ *This building was destroyed by a hurricane in 2005.*

In 2005 Hurricane Wilma damaged hotels and businesses. Vacationers could not visit here. This harmed Mexico's **tourist industry**.

Preparing for a Hurricane

Weather forecasters can see a hurricane forming and moving in photographs taken by **satellites** in space. The hurricane's cloud moves in a **spiral** over the Earth.

■ *This woman is checking the latest satellite photographs to see if a hurricane is forming.*

Television, radio, and the Internet warn people before the hurricane strikes. On the **coast**, special flags are sometimes used to warn people that a hurricane is on the way.

■ *Red flags warn people to find safety.*

Coping with Hurricanes

People often nail strong wooden boards in front of doors and windows before a hurricane strikes. This stops the hurricane's winds from smashing the glass.

■ *People protect their homes when they know a hurricane is coming.*

■ *It is sometimes safer to leave home before a hurricane hits.*

Many people go to community centers or special **shelters** before a hurricane hits. They are given food and a place to sleep. They stay until the hurricane is over and it is safe to go home.

Hurricane Katrina

Hurricane Katrina hit the United States in 2005. It caused terrible floods in the city of New Orleans.

■ *Hurricane Katrina flooded city streets.*

Thousands of people had to leave their homes. Katrina caused more damage than any other hurricane in U.S. history.

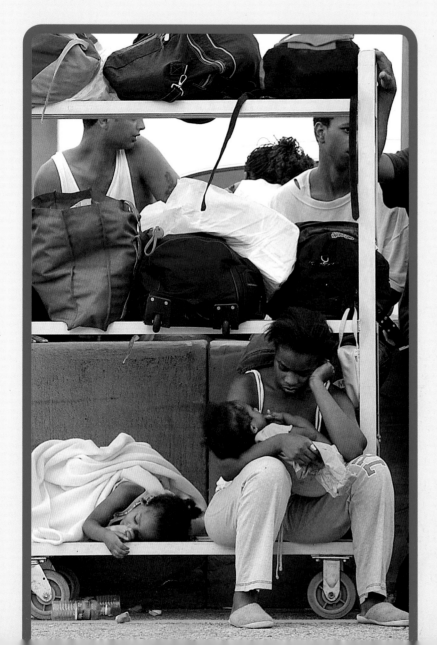

■ *These people were made homeless by Hurricane Katrina.*

Nature and Hurricanes

Hurricane winds and rain can destroy **crops**. In poor countries, such as Bangladesh, these crops are very important. If they are destroyed, people will not have enough to eat.

Asia

Bangladesh

Pacific Ocean

Africa

Indian Ocean

Australia

■ *Crops can be destroyed by floods.*

■ *The way palm trees grow helps them to survive hurricanes.*

Palm trees grow in the **Tropics**. These trees can bend and sway without breaking. They can survive very strong winds.

To the Rescue!

Some people cannot get to safe places during hurricanes. Rescuers find people buried under fallen houses and trailers. Trailers get damaged easily by the strong winds.

■ *These men are rescuing people from mud after a hurricane.*

■ *After a hurricane it is important to have fresh water supplies.*

Hurricane rains **flood** drains and water supplies. This makes the water dirty. Dirty drinking water can cause **diseases**. So **aid workers** bring in fresh water, as well as food.

Adapting to Hurricanes

Belize is a country in Central America. A hurricane destroyed its **capital city**, which lay on the **coast**. This picture shows the new city.

■ *The new city was built inland, well away from hurricanes.*

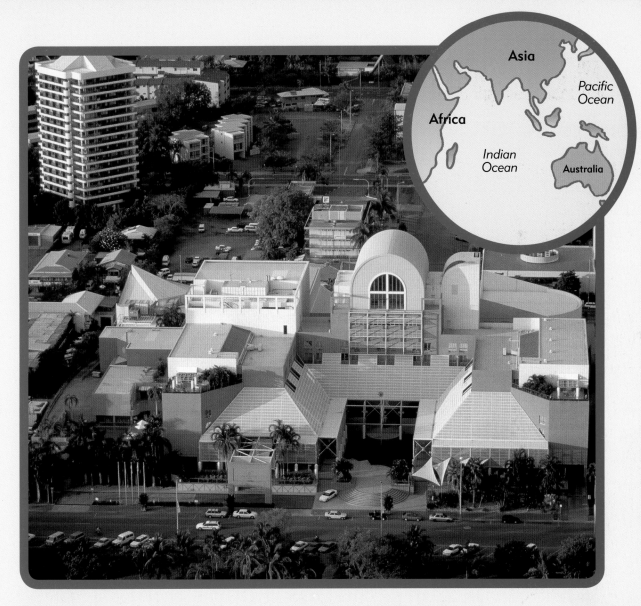

Asia

Pacific
Ocean

Africa

Indian
Ocean

Australia

■ *Buildings in a hurricane zone must be specially designed.*

Parts of Australia lie in a **hurricane zone**.
People now have to build stronger buildings
that will not be destroyed in a hurricane.

Fact File

◆ The worst known hurricane disaster happened in the country of Bangladesh in 1970. About 500,000 people died.

◆ There is a small area of calm air in the center of a hurricane. This place is called the "eye" of the storm.

◆ Hurricanes are given names, such as Andrew or Katrina. Their names go in alphabetical order. If one hurricane has a boy's name, then the next one is given a girl's name.

Glossary

aid worker worker who helps people in a disaster

capital city most important city of a country, where the government meets

coast where the land meets the sea

crop plant grown for food

disease illness

flood overflow of water onto land that is usually dry

hurricane zone area where hurricanes often happen

mass large amount of something like air that does not have a definite shape

ocean one of the four large bodies of salt water that cover Earth

pressure pushing force

satellite spacecraft that travels around Earth

shelter safe place

shore where the sea meets the land

spiral shape that is made by circling around a center point

storm surge huge sea wave pushed to the shore by hurricane winds

tourist industry businesses where people on vacation pay to visit or stay

Tropics very warm, wet areas of the world near the Equator

weather forecaster scientist who works out what the weather will be like

More Books to Read

Mayer, Cassie. *Weather Watchers: Wind*. Chicago: Heinemann Library, 2006

Royston, Angela. *The Weather: Wind*. Mankato, Minn.: Chrysalis Children's Books, 2004

Index